FAVORITE
BASEBALL
★ TEAMS ★

LOS ANGELES

DODGERS

BY K. C. KELLEY

The Child's World

Published by The Child's World®
1980 Lookout Drive • Mankato, MN 56003-1705
800-599-READ • www.childsworld.com

ACKNOWLEDGMENTS
The Child's World®: Mary Berendes,
    Publishing Director
The Design Lab: Kathleen Petelinsek, Design
Shoreline Publishing Group, LLC: James
    Buckley Jr., Production Director

PHOTOS
Cover: Focus on Baseball
Interior: All photos by Focus on Baseball except:
AP/Wide World: 10, 17, 21, 22; Getty: 5, 13.

LIBRARY OF CONGRESS
CATALOGING-IN-PUBLICATION DATA
Kelley, K. C.
  Los Angeles Dodgers / by K.C. Kelley.
    p. cm. — (Favorite baseball teams)
  Includes index.
  ISBN 978-1-60253-378-3 (library bound : alk. paper)
  1. Los Angeles Dodgers (Baseball team)—Juvenile
literature. I. Title. II. Series.
  GV875.L6K45 2010
  796.357'640979494—dc22   2009040097

Printed in the United States of America
Mankato, Minnesota
November 2009
F11460

On the cover: Matt Kemp, Outfield

CONTENTS

Go, Dodgers!

The Dodgers have always been one of baseball's most popular teams. In their first home in Brooklyn, New York, everyone loved them. Now they are in Los Angeles, and they are a big part of the city. Fans love them there, too! The Dodgers reward their fans with lots of wins. The team has won five **World Series**! Let's meet the Dodgers.

Dodgers games often include stars from TV, movies, or music. ▶
Singing star Cherice kicked off Opening Day in 2009.

Who Are the Dodgers?

The Los Angeles Dodgers are a team in baseball's National League (N.L.). The N.L. joins with the American League (A.L.) to form Major League Baseball. The Dodgers play in the West Division of the N.L. The division winners get to play in the league playoffs. The playoff winners from the two leagues face off in the World Series. The Dodgers have won five World Series championships.

◀ Bat and ball meet perfectly in this swing by Dodgers second baseman Orlando "O-Dog" Hudson.

Where They Came From

The Dodgers have been around for a long time. The team was formed in 1884. They weren't called the Dodgers, though. They were called the Bridegrooms, then the Robins, and then the Superbas. Their name today comes from "Trolley Dodgers." A trolley is a kind of streetcar. People in Brooklyn had to dodge the trolleys when crossing streets! In 1959, the team moved to Los Angeles. People in Brooklyn were very sad. People in L.A. were very excited!

The Dodgers' home in Brooklyn was Ebbets Field. ▶

Who They Play

The Los Angeles Dodgers play 162 games each season. That includes about 18 games against the other teams in their division, the N.L. West. The Dodgers have won 12 N.L. West championships. The other N.L. West teams are the Arizona Diamondbacks, the San Diego Padres, and the San Francisco Giants. The Dodgers and the Giants have a long **rivalry**. They used to play each other when they were both in New York. They still play big games every year! The Dodgers also play some teams from the American League. Their A.L. **opponents** change every year.

◀ Crash! He's out! Games between the Dodgers and the Giants are always very exciting.

Where They Play

Dodger Stadium is one of baseball's best places to watch a game. The weather is always nice, and the stadium is always bright and clean. Dodger Stadium is also ringed with palm trees. The Dodgers' fans pack the place all the time. The team has had more than 3 million fans in 23 seasons!

Fans dressed in blue and white enjoy great baseball in the California sunshine! ▶

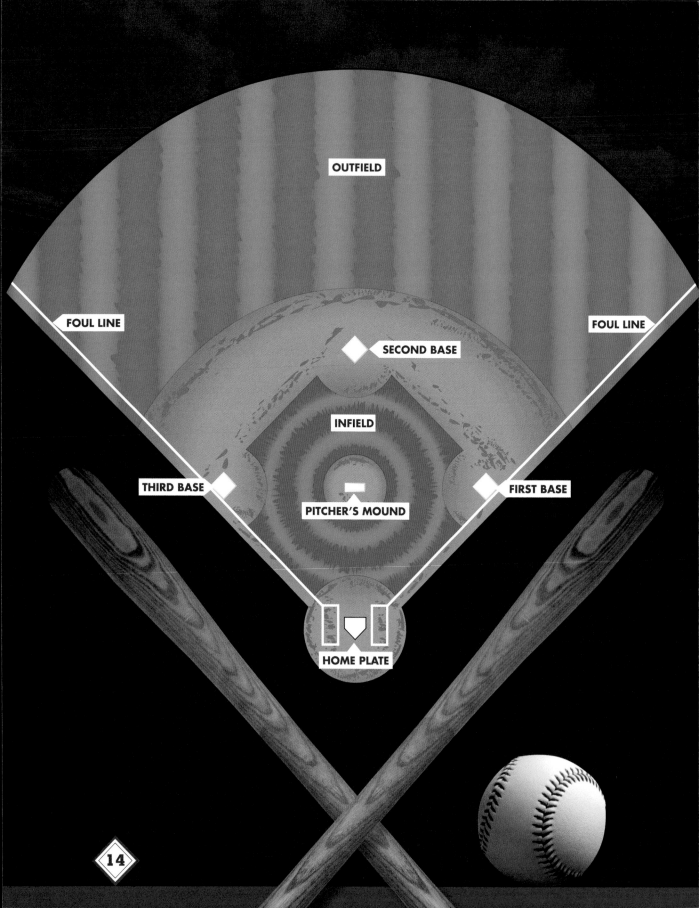

The Baseball Diamond

Baseball games are played on a diamond. Four bases form this diamond shape. The bases are 90 feet (27 m) apart. The area around the bases is called the **infield**. At the center of the infield is the pitcher's mound. The grass area beyond the bases is called the **outfield**. White lines start at **home plate** and go toward the outfield. These are the foul lines. Baseballs hit outside these lines are out of play. The outfield walls are about 300-450 feet (91-137 m) from home plate.

Big Days!

The Dodgers have had some great seasons in their history. Here are three of the best:

1955: The Dodgers had lost seven World Series. But finally, they won one! They beat their crosstown rivals, the New York Yankees. Fans all over Brooklyn celebrated!

1963: Led by ace pitcher Sandy Koufax, the Dodgers won their second World Series in L.A. They beat the Yankees again.

1988: Kirk Gibson hit a famous ninth-inning homer to win Game 1 of the World Series. The Dodgers then won three more games to beat the Oakland A's!

General manager Fred Claire and **manager** Tommy Lasorda lift the ▸
1988 World Series championship trophy.

Tough Days!

Not every season can end with a World Series win. Here are some of the toughest seasons in Dodgers history:

1905: They were called the Brooklyn Superbas. But they weren't **superb** this year! They lost a team-record 104 games.

1978: The Dodgers were doing well, but they couldn't win the big one. They lost the World Series for the third time in six seasons!

1992: The Dodgers finished last in the N.L. West for the only time in their history!

◄ Dodgers manager Tommy Lasorda and first baseman Steve Garvey can't bear to watch their team lose the 1978 World Series.

Meet the Fans

Dodgers fans love their team! Lots and lots of people come to the games. Dodgers fans sometimes get to the games late. Traffic in Los Angeles is very busy! But once they're in their seats at Dodger Stadium, they love to yell for their team. If you go to a game, look for beach balls bouncing around the stands.

Dodgers fans love manager Joe Torre so much they joined his family ▶ in wishing him a happy birthday in 2009!

Sandy Koufax, Pitcher

22

Heroes Then . . .

Zach Wheat and Babe Herman were great outfielders for the Dodgers in the early 1900s. Jackie Robinson was a great infielder in the 1950s. He was also the first African-American player in baseball in more than 50 years. His courage helped change America. Shortstop Pee Wee Reese helped welcome Jackie to the team. Pee Wee was also a great fielder and leader. Center fielder Duke Snider was a powerful slugger. Pitcher Sandy Koufax was baseball's best in the 1960s. He won three **Cy Young Awards** and set records for most strikeouts. In the 1970s, first baseman Steve Garvey helped the team reach three World Series. Pitcher Orel Hershiser was the **Most Valuable Player (MVP)** of the 1988 World Series.

◀ Jackie Robinson was one of baseball's bravest and best players.
Inset: Sandy Koufax was the top pitcher of the 1960s.

Heroes Now . . .

The Dodgers have some of baseball's best young stars. Outfielders Andre Ethier and James Loney are great fielders and hitters. Catcher Russell Martin helps lead a super pitching staff. Second baseman Orlando "O-Dog" Hudson is becoming a top hitter. Starting pitcher Chad Billingsley was an **All-Star**. Relief pitcher Jonathan Broxton is one of baseball's fastest pitchers.

Chad Billingsley, Pitcher

Russell Martin, Catcher

Andre Ethier, Outfield

BATTING HELMET

TEAM JERSEY

UNDERSHIRT

BATTING GLOVE

BAT

TEAM PANTS

CATCHER'S CHEST PROTECTOR

CATCHER'S MASK

CATCHER'S MITT

CATCHER'S SHIN GUARD

Russell Martin, Catcher

BASEBALL CLEATS

Gearing Up

Baseball players all wear a team jersey and pants. They have to wear a team hat in the field and a helmet when batting. Take a look at Matt Kemp and Russell Martin to see some other parts of a baseball player's uniform.

THE BASEBALL

A Major League baseball weighs about 5 ounces (142 g). It is 9 inches (23 cm) around. A leather cover surrounds hundreds of feet of string. That string is wound around a small center of rubber and cork.

SPORTS STATS

Here are some all-time career records for the Los Angeles Dodgers. All the stats are through the 2009 season.

HOME RUNS

Duke Snider, 389

Gil Hodges, 361

RUNS BATTED IN

Duke Snider, 1,271

Gil Hodges, 1,254

BATTING AVERAGE

Babe Herman, .339

Mike Piazza, .331

WINS BY A PITCHER

Don Sutton, 233
Don Drysdale, 209

STOLEN BASES

Maury Wills, 490
Davey Lopes, 418

WINS BY A MANAGER

Walter Alson, 2,040

EARNED RUN AVERAGE

Jeff Pfeffer, 2.31
Nap Rucker, 2.42

Glossary

All-Star a player who is named as one of the league's best and plays in the All-Star Game between the A.L. and the N.L.

Cy Young Award an award given to the top pitcher in each league

general manager a person who works off the field for a baseball team to choose players and hire the manager

home plate a five-sided rubber pad where batters stand to swing, and where runners touch base to score runs

infield the area around and between the four bases of a baseball diamond

manager the person who is in charge of the team and chooses who will bat and pitch

Most Valuable Player (MVP) a yearly award given to the top player in each league

opponents teams or players that play against each other

outfield the large, grass area beyond the infield of a baseball diamond

rivalry an ongoing competition between teams that play each other often, over a long time

superb excellent, outstanding

World Series the Major League Baseball championship, played each year between the winners of the American and National Leagues

Find Out More

BOOKS

Buckley, James Jr. *Eyewitness Baseball*. New York: DK Publishing, 2010.

Prince, April Jones. *Jackie Robinson: He Led the Way*. New York: Grosset & Dunlap, 2007.

Stewart, Mark. *Los Angeles Dodgers*. Chicago: Norwood House Press, 2008.

Teitelbaum, Michael. *Baseball*. Ann Arbor, MI: Cherry Lake Publishing, 2009.

WEB SITES

Visit our Web page for links about the Los Angeles Dodgers and other pro baseball teams.

childsworld.com/links

Note to Parents, Teachers, and Librarians: We routinely verify our Web links to make sure they are safe, active sites—so encourage your readers to check them out!

Index

ABOUT THE AUTHOR

K.C. Kelley has written dozens of books on baseball and other sports for young readers. He has also been a youth baseball coach and called baseball games on the radio. His favorite team? The Boston Red Sox.